Beneath the Blue

by Karishma Natu

for the boy i last loved.

i hope you learn to love yourself before letting
another good woman walk out of your life.

table of contents

dawn

7:12am behind the door
what's the plan?
beach sunrise
are we there yet?
she's here

morning

i ask for coffee and i'm asking too much
stop dreaming, you just slept
so poetic for no reason, oh my god
sky: a table set each morning
between you and me
parents
summer, be it a season or so

afternoon

"yeah, you'll get there! *tumbleweed rolls
past*
the architect
to be a young woman taking the train
home
second to run
corner shop
receipts
mid-june and life is changing
butterfly wings

dusk	pearls
	she
	keepsakes that could've been
	a thank you to my first friend (D.C)
	beneath the blue
	l'heure bleue
	september waits
	paint
	reruns of you and i
	left, in the wilderness
night	the poet's cake
	atoms of the sky
	april showers
	midnight hour
	stargaze
	always at 52
	itch i can't scratch
	forsaken
	stars aren't strangers
	so this is twenty-one
	a first time for everything
midnight	midnights, camera, action.
	between me and you
	late
	the sensitive one
	immortalised

dawn

7:12am behind the door

daylight peeks in to ask if i'm awake,
    shedding across vanilla speckled sheets. the
cotton wrinkles mark my forearms.

i tie the morning's downpour of curls;
    they are still deep in slumber, windswept
by the atmosphere in dreams.

again my notebook lays patient;
    she waits for me each day in hopes she will
spend an arduous date with her favourite pen.

me and my room open eyes
    like a turned sheet page made for orchestra,
ready to compose another song.

what's the plan?

i didn't plan on you.
i didn't plan on falling as fast
or as far as i did,
but it might be the best thing i've done.

three years of building a life of my own have taught me
i didn't plan on consuming bucket-tons of mango,
learning how to tango,
falling off a bike in stasis,
or familarising myself with life's divinest faces.

i certainly didn't plan on you,
just as night never planned on dawn,
yet how lucky the moon is to fall into
shy clouds of day.

nothing is innately planned.
somehow it's easy to assume
everything should be.
when writing rules your life,
you get used to risks.

writers don't act according to time,
we grasp emptiness and fulfilment of single seconds.
we're here to lose at life again and again
and run the longer road to win it.

this wasn't part of the plan and it never will be.
a plan is a list of things that will get me to
where i need to be.
i already feel content with you.
with all of this.
i don't plan on stopping.

beach sunrise

beach sunrise.
push and pull tide
you and i
lived in each others bedrooms
now we live out of each other's lives.

on the phone,
you told me you wanted to be
the man i fell in love with
but i just wanted to be
your woman.

your silence shrinks me
yet you drown me out with complacency.

i was the thrill in your double-edged act.
i didn't become a girlfriend,
i became someone you wanted to hide.
i became someone who watered your excuses,
hesitant to pull out weeds and say goodbye.

i'm sorry i still think i'm going to wake up
and be met with your eyes.
do you regret that after all that time
living in each others bedrooms
and in each other's lives,
we never caught
the beach sunrise?

are we there yet?

time isn't measured in minutes,
until you're so "bored" or "busy" that you give it a name.

it takes two to brush your teeth
and even less to tell someone how you feel.
these days, i don't know which gives me higher points in the game.

it takes five hours, maybe days, to read a book
but it takes three when it remains gripping a post-narrative hook.

it takes a couple hours to watch something,
to dedicate your attention to a reality that isn't yours
which also and therefore isn't mine.
how many people spend more hours watching the same thing,
watching dumb shit or "how to fix" everything online,
spending a lifetime on creating voids to avoid vulnerability?
a youthful coping strategy for instability
in every sense of the word.

we fork out our time getting to know every ending
of every story,
to lessen the severity of our own.

i don't want to (and my biggest fear is to) get to forty,
when i was twenty yesterday,
and talk of all the ways i could've grown, wondering why i wasted most of
my nights
validating myself with "self care" when i was really just fucking
alone.

i'm quite sorry to want to make the most of it.
to nestle in every corner of my life that i can fit,
never to stay in the middle.
i ache to learn, but i must love and lose.

time isn't measured in minutes
it is measured in moments we can't choose.

14

she's here

people ask why i like the rain so much.
i think of quieter times, the times when we'd have to stay inside at school
and instead of playing the board games my friends wanted me to,
i would sit and write.
the world slows when it rains.
we think of duvet days and "things to do when it's grey,"
how we can make ourselves warm and cozy when the weather is cold and wet.
autumn is sisters with silence.
it's eloquent, even.
i've missed this.

morning

i ask for coffee and i'm asking too much

i'll take a cinnamon honey flat white
to cope with the heaviness; let it be a cure.
i never liked this time of year.
oh, £3.65, sure.

my pockets are filled with tiny bits of tissue
and my heart is dragging along the floor.
it's only eight forty-four,
but it already feels like i've been here for years.

the weather? yeah i know too well.
and i hope you know how hard it is to live here,
to live here,
when your dreams depend on somewhere else
entirely,
not somewhere in holiday-getaway hell.

i am still aching from july
and the agony of it all.
does the place i was born
automatically make me a fly
on the wall?

i suppose so. i suppose i had a choice
to stay;
be homeless and happy with living that way.
for the sake of not being in this awful place,
where it's fact that ambition comes to die.
i'm trying,
             i'm trying,
                          i'm trying
to get by.

chocolate dust ? oh, yes please.
thanks.
have a nice day.
and just like that, another goodbye
august is always bittersweet that way.

one in four adults skip breakfast most days. some call it pointless.

breakfast is my favourite.
each day when the curtains
tell me it's time to get up,
i open them.
i watch them hang dejectedly
like the clouds i frequently ignore.
they watch me drown in a blush of blue sky.

anyways, i eat granola, blueberries and yogurt.
some call it fancy.
truth be told, i'm always hungry for
words i haven't yet tasted.

i suppose it is terribly sad to live here
in a room made for mornings.
beautiful poetry is curious of night-
about the universe, politics, and places.
it seems my pen desires daylight;
coffee, cream, a spoonful of spring.
i call it art. some call it cliché.

say, "couldn't do what you do,"
yet scoff at delicate articulation.

as if "poetic" must be expelled,
like it's monday morning.
as if it lingered like garlic upon breath.
as if you wouldn't be caught DEAD
with the way it sits on your lips,
even though it tastes undeniably good.

literature, you say, *hobby*.
language, you say, talking.
metaphor, all i've known, easier than walking.

my brain, bless it, poor thing,
is rotting with apology.
a poetic-clusterfuck anomaly
shut down for emotional transparency.

say, "that's piss easy, that,"
yet scoff at intelligent articulation.

how could i show a gallery of intricate paintings
to people who say it's just shapes and colours?
how could i unlearn the thing that keeps me alive
for the sake of a few others?

square by square,
sort of frayed at the edges,
loose threads belong to only I,
tablecloth.

grey with the weight of it all,
overcast mounds my delicacy
every breakfast, every time
the Gods joyously spoon generous
amounts of daylight onto their plates,
filled with teal, aqua, baby blue.

what use would I be without them?

well, I'd sit here looking pretty for the world.

what would they do without me?
they'd simply-
find a new tablecloth.

for the life of me,
i cannot remember a time i could breathe,
escaping with the wind,
without being held in place
or being spilled upon with water
accidentally.

between you and me

kindled,
caramelised.
each breath a flourishing flame.
it seems we both crave
saccharinity
in one another's company.

eyes glazing over skin,
treacled adoration of amber.
his fingertips like delicate rays,
lips pecking each speck on my face;
the scatter of
vanilla bean freckles.

parents

pears no longer grow on the neighbour's tree.
my bowls have been moved to the back of the cupboard
and my bedroom is a cardboard box gallery.
my roots were planted here but no longer serve me.

there's loose change on the coffee table and open drawers.
mum washes up and spills a rapture of suds on the floor,
papa helps her with a mountain of kitchen towels.
i notice my parents have always been and are only human now.

i'm outside writing because i'm rivals with rest.
through the window, papa puts his thumbs up at me,
holding up his third glass of water today.
i was ten five minutes ago and in the mirror this morning
i found more than three greys.

there's yoghurt in the fridge from last time i was here;
because my parents will hold onto anything so i don't disappear.

summer, be it a season or so

july has wallowed in gloom
beside handfuls of farewells.

nobody asked you to
pour coffee, heart dripping down your sleeve.
masterpiece after masterpiece, as if
you'd handpicked each bean
before grinding them to granules.

nobody asked you to,
and you couldn't have seen,
but you loved me everywhere-
even around the rims and broken seams
belonging to the room in my chest.

for days to come, my memories will spill
from heart onto page,
along with sunset lattes and the mellowness
of being known by favourite flavours,
even if this was a fleeting stay.

you've been good to know.
though i'm leaving you behind
i'm not worried;
your care has safely walked me home.

this must be it then,
a bittersweet goodbye.
though i'm two hours down the road
i know now that i'm never alone.

afternoon

many, many, many possibilities.
couldn't count on two hands.

i'm getting too old to stay young.
soon, skies will feel less like a roof
and more like the porch
of a house i can no longer live in.

last time
i stepped foot on the beach i left
a girl who devoted her life
to being a student.

lingering half-undone,
i find i am left with sad sickly sand
and a handful of waves goodbye
that'll push me five steps
behind.

many, many, many possibilities.
couldn't count them on two hands.
but every chance you take on a possibility
is one step closer than you-
or anyone- thinks.

how do you build a home
bound by the judgement of everyone else?

the dream?
you ask.
pinterest-inspired.
minimalist, pristine oak floors.
tiny home. bathroom, 4 by 4.
daintily cottagecore.
something that'll have my house tour
trending on youtube.

the dream?
you ask.
mid-century modern.
big windows but big blinds as to not be seen,
a kitchen smothered by sage green,
an l-shaped sofa with cloud pillows of lilac and cream,
yeah, that's th-

the dream?
you (didn't) ask.
four walls of your time
and a mug full of tea,
fairy lights that delicately sit in the hallway.
showers of uninterrupted company.
cushioned carpet, lemon curd toast,
head over shoulder, face to chest scenery.

the stable structure of a hug;
a place beyond a welcome rug.

perhaps a house is not a home
until it has been lived in,
and a dream is just a fantasy
until it is past being drawn.
until it is being built.

until it is full of life;
one you might call your own.

a home is made
when you're not searching for one,
right outside your door.

to be a young woman taking the train home

a woman opposite me fends tears;
she stares off into splatters of greenery,
twenty something too.
i wonder if she feels so much less
when she couldn't be any more.

i wonder if she'r   hone
heartbeat of t
sound of th
slow and sle
of her favou

i wonder if a
thanked her f

we have someth
neither of us will n.
and if we are,
soon is too far.

it seems youth's full stop is a tr
dancing in the flames of naïvety.

a woman opposite me hugs her bag,
she stares off into the big wide world,
once something-teen too.
i wonder if she feels so much less
when she couldn't be any more.

34

are you there
                              standing somewhere in the shadows?

maybe it's me,

casted as   hesitation.

the option you linger   on for far too long.

a silver medal decorated so daintily
in ruffles of dust.

                        take me down, if you must.

it is unlikely the sun will greet my skin.

how dare i sit here,   rotting to my pit,   feeling like i lost
even each time i won?

how could i be content, how could i find hope
how could i   run

after all you haven't done?

absence becomes a debt unpayable.
it is home to me.
i am never first,
but i can no longer live
                        second best.

corner shop

the shop owner asks if i'm okay and i feel perhaps
as if i began falling years back in stilettos, as if almost
every version of myself collapsed.

i want to tell him i'm sad, scared, and a little lost.
maybe he could tell me where to go,
maybe that's why our paths crossed.

i'm 5 foot small.
he folds an open cardboard box. smiles
because that's all
he's ever known.

i pick up double chocolate chip
Maryland cookies. they remind me of momentary
glimpses of childhood with my brother; corner shop trips
days before he grew up.

long before he knew his lifelong dream
wasn't meant for him.
long before i knew my lifelong dream
would always revolve around synonyms.

part of me wants to buy a magazine, but they no longer
have cheap plastic rings with gem stickers in them.

part of me wants to hold £2 in my hand
like i did back then, the coins listening to
mine and my brother's chit-chat worth more than a grand
and i'd ask if he brought the sonic screwdriver
just in case we'd need it at hand

the shop owner asks if i'm okay, and i want to say
it doesn't snow anymore, i wonder why.
getting snowballs thrown at by my brother was
one of the only good ways to cry.

when i go to pay i talk to the shop owner
about uni. he congratulates me the way parents do.
and i turn to pick up a can of diet coke
because i'm a big girl now.

the item i brought back home
that held the most value
was the smile the shopkeeper gave me
despite being so alone.

at the bottom of my bag sat the reminder
that every interaction, no matter how long or temporary,
can make an entire day.
enough of them can make an *entire lifetime.*

receipts

june gently rolls into bites
of soft serve diligence,
spoonfuls of
nice to meet you's and second-to-last goodbyes.
i am left with pocketfuls of crumpled paper.

my colleague carries an
effervescence, a brightness that could never douse.
she tells me, beaming, about this place
you can visit in india,
to turn in receipts for rupees.

we eye the stack of receipts on the counter,
and she picks it up like it's a luxury holiday in her hands.

"should we trade them in?"
i half-joke.

spending what had served purpose elsewhere
on something worthwhile
might be a plan.
i think tonight i'll pack my things.

receipts are yours to keep
unless you don't want them.
they float free;
intricately printed and full of value.
if you bury them until they're truly alone,
they'll have better places to be.

lately i've been carrying synonyms in my pocket,
but they turn to torn-up tissue when i'm talking.
today i took the train back,
carried my boxes with open lids.

GWR ticket lady scans my ticket
and obviously her heart was left somewhere down the tracks.
i hope she doesn't see my eyes begin to confess my fears- then again- what
can she do?

little lumps form a herd of pent tears,
then linger in the back of my throat as i stare out of the cookie-cut window,
listening to 'fine line' by harry styles
to *reminisce the concert*, i tell myself,
though i've looped it at least fourteen times.

i am here with too many people,
in particular an old couple who are dreadfully dampened
by a singular cloud in the sky.

it's june and i am sick with summer.
all the promises of the past
and an already forgotten future
wash me away completely, and i can't swim, so naturally, i drown.

everyone seems to think this is lots of fun.

firefly wings

let's make rain angels-
our gliding limbs
won't leave a print
but we'll end up laughing
carelessly.
like we have plenty of puddles left
to jump into,

and according to you,
this is the first episode
of our series.
see, we don't meet much;
life tends to drop branches in our way.
glitter dances across apricot skies rarely
because true peace is a guest,
not something blue, not appearing everyday.

it is something you hope to see soon.
being with you is a gifted afternoon.
our conversation flies
like it is sat on a tree hung swing.
you bring my favourite kind of safety;
a safety not many people could bring.

you are the first day of spring.
and our friendship gives us firefly wings.
it has no end and it has just begun.
our friendship is a dainty float
across the setting sun.

dusk

pearls

and here's me-
characterised by blame,
looking for a miracle
in the mirror again.
all choked up
because at least she would be proud-
that little girl i once was
who ended up lost, then found.

found-
and bound- by
water,
dancing around my ankles;
how its freshness flirted with my breath.

the water, he
became too much of an interference
at best.
then, silently tumultuous
at worst.

i guess he gave me pretty things
like shells.

i became chewed up between ripples
and all the waves could do were
look at me with straight faced sentimentality
and pocketfuls of washed up agony
ready for someone delicate to deal with.

what i wanted to say was,

"but it's not mine it's yours."

to climb down from the clouds
and give it all back.

yet how the thunder impressed him,
how the lightning gave him something
to work with,
how the rain added
dramatic effect.

before, i showed the sea my prettiest
colours at sunset.
he would look at me like he couldn't believe i existed,
then i'd watch him become a

mirror,

so i could never dive
beneath the

water.

to be a woman is
to be prized.
to hurt as a woman
is to not be seen
but try to tell them you're still
somehow alive.
to be a woman is
to be prized.

and here's me-
characterised by a storm.
and there's you-
taking pride
in the fact that you don't need to
conform.

i guess we're told he can give us pretty things
like pearls.

she,
me; as poet,
as daughter,
as woman,
will build a home with
the lines of an a5 page.
furnishing it with words
that belong to a twenty-one year old sensitive heart,
finding the cherishing arms of art

i will build chairs to support
my spine,
made to snap your perception of me.
putting a splinter in expectations;
refined to what i can finally call mine
without a single hesitation.

i, me;
as poet,
as sister,
as woman,
will lay bricks
cemented in glorious worth
drawing strength from each corner of this earth

i-

I,

will rise after every fall,
outrun every chance to crawl,
i, for one, for one hundred
for my grandmother,
for the girl who always borrowed my hairbands,
for my beautiful friends who's smiles could light a million streets,
for you,
for me,

for our cries, for our calls,
for you,
for we,
should never dare to remain
small.

keepsakes that could've been

if i had to count
a penny for each moment we didn't
live out then maybe
it would cost
a lifetime.

an aggravating longing
for my youth will arise
and occur more frequently
than just missing it. how do you ever
get to be okay with that?

okay with my name lingering
just beneath the tongue? okay with leaving
open doors, expecting nobody to walk through?
okay with thinking i might've closed it?

all these possibilities add up
to absolutely nothing at all,
because if they weren't once just
possibilities, perhaps
they'd be everything to me now.

a thank you for my first friend, (d.c.)

did you know there's a shortcut?
follow the path of magnolias
sitting damp from the rain, in sympathy
of all the times i've walked here and cried.
think of all the autumn glazed evenings i've failed but tried
to fit into your pair of size 9 shoes.

our names are still carved on the shelter
in the park.
i wonder if you ever look for them.

i wonder if you're reminded of muddy trainers,
conversation curling into fields of rolled butter,
chomping on oreo bites quicker than clouds turn to stars.

life then was a nose stuffed with freshly-mowed grass
and chewed-up and spat-out conundrums.

trees aren't so easy to climb now we've lived
the years we often prayed to pass us by.

i miss tiptoeing on the honeyed miserable carpet in your house.

perhaps i'll knock for you sometime.

i make a list of
all the things i want to share with you;

all the orange segments and apple slices,
early one-more-minute eyes
sunlight entices.

spoonfuls of food you made too spicy for you
so it was perfect for me,
birthday cake on paper plates,
kisses of maple syrup on pancake dates.

all stained wooden spoons making a kitchen home,
all ever-gentle phone calls from down the road
to further away,
and all things devastatingly mundane i've ever wanted to say.

i've out-sprinted the arms of clocks
to lace fingers, to taste moments of your love in lilac.
you said every place i'm in is your safe place
when i held you sleepy,
tracing hearts on your back (without you realising).

i want to clap for as long as i have hands
whenever you take a bow.
i want to walk into a crowded room,
gaze falling upon you first anyhow.

along with my stomach butterflies,
i aspire to stay curious sans choice.
they're always fluttering, asking
when you'll catch them
with your honey-varnished voice.

because there is nothing i ache for more
than the gentle legato of you talking.
when i'm with you i feel

like all i've known is flying, not walking.

so i'll continue wishing
on each star, each 11:11, for us to be true.
nightly, you're a sunset reminding me
there is much more beneath the sky's
shifting shades of blue.

i made a list of
all of my favourite things about you.
i am convinced it will be endless.
i am convinced that i love you,

through and through and through.

l'heure bleue

once a little girl,

from the ground of open, silent country road,
wishing on stars,
gut-punched nothing ever came true.

now, bathed in blue
beside someone it adorns ever so beautifully,
stars aligned and all.

dusted in january's mist,
looking more beautiful on you than it has ever.
i jump a puddle the size of a pond,
and you give me the first look
of many.

a look that says,
i'd like to share these sunsets with you,
one way or another.

you were wearing that emerald coat,
the one you took ages to put on in your short film,
and the one you later showed up in at 1am
to deliver me eggs because the neighbourhood cat ate my cake.
it sits on your shoulders like it was made for you.
it still does.
perhaps it always will.

twiddling thumbs
and conversations in our reflections on the tube.
time that ticks out of nowhere into twilight.
in paris, they call this l'eure bleue.

i don't care how many laps i run in my life,
if i don't see your face each time i go around,
i don't know how i'll make it to the finish line.

once alone,
now i'm grown, and have someone to call
mine.

september waits

sunset trickles through train windows.
the blue; the grey, gallops into a blush
of marigold and rose.
i suppose woollen clouds will keep me warm
in the breeze between

august and seeing you.
how do you flourish in patience
without holding a breath?
perhaps there will forever be fireworks
twirling out from our chests,
whether miles apart or my head finds your shoulder.

august and we're holding hands,
fingertips ripple upon skin
like delicate drops of summer rain.
we hide from typical british weather
just to sneak some more kisses again.

august and it is you.
it is you and i am sentimental with certainty,
just as i have been since i wrote
"i can't stop smiling what is this"
in my notes app that night we stayed up until 1am talking.
just as i have been since winter's glistening sun
melted in your eyes while we spent four hours walking.

since spilling jokes over coffee,
and since you said your hair was ruined by wind
but i dared to and will never not disagree.

august and it is you.
beyond the stunning skies,
you are by far my favourite view.
woollen clouds will keep me warm
between august

and seeing you.

ceiling to floor,
we paint in the shade "bittersweet."
i fall for you minute by minute and
each second is a treat.
it's a beautiful complexity;
a glittering blend of roseate and ivory.

it looks like inescapable laugher and
a gardener's blissful day.
it looks like two twirling butterflies
in the meadow of things you say.
it tastes like meringue kisses and
brightens the room like years
of shooting star wishes.

yesterday the room was full of wonder
and tomorrow it will be painted in the shade
 "something missing."

ceiling to floor,
i lived in that space with you
for twenty four hours and never
again.
i pack up the clothes that you held me in
and i pack up my tears because it'll be fine,
for we'll see each other who-knows-when.

ceiling to floor,
i paint the walls around me "white,"
for a room without you
means almost nothing at all.

next time, i will leave my notebook in your pocket
so that when you come back
i know where to find
all the words i lost when i last looked in your eyes.

so that you can carry
my love for you
wherever you go
for however long we are apart.

let my love have your mornings,
afternoons, sunsets.

with each visit,
i'll stamp it for you;
seal it with a kiss,
and maybe

this time, will you leave your camera in my pocket
so that when i come back
you know where to find
the places you captured
before you got lost in my eyes?

our safety net is scattered,
loose pinpoints on a map.
what do they call this?
the feeling of not belonging somewhere,
only to a few people?

friendship.
smells like half split clementines and
the ocean's deepest breath at sunsets.
i'm waiting for a sombre sky
let me, let me, let me inside
i'm walking the streets like a stray
not home, not home, not home, away

then a string of three
run to cradle me
like cubs protecting their sibling.

a benevolent paw wipes tears,
another caresses my hair,
one has eyes that well up with care
but they also dart
in a way that says 'beware.'

i lay, still sore
from the heartache of it all
playing connect the dots
below a sheet of stars,
lucky to even have the floor.

the three make sure
to say that a roar can keep me safe
and when silence must cease to exist,
i will wear a heart nobody could chafe.

our safety net is scattered,
loose pinpoints on a map.
what do they call this?
the feeling of not belonging somewhere,
only to a few people?

night

atoms of the sky

if our atoms were before us,
i wonder if they crossed paths.
after all, the chances that they are here together now
are smaller than anything anyone could see.
if our atoms were before us,
our togetherness may have been clearer than life itself.

i lay beside you at night,
glimpses of being awake,
our closeness fosters kisses for just seconds
in between rest.
from memory, softly,
easily, we find each others lips in the dark
like we know of nothing else in our sleepy state.

i fall into gentle slumber at the thought
of your hand over my head covering me from the rain.
i think about the way our thumbs often mingle,
holding a conversation whenever we sit beside one another in silence.

i look at you and you tell me you can't believe
you got so lucky.
i can't believe he thinks he is lucky.
after all, aren't we both?
to even exist at the same time
and to have met when the universe said
it was right?

if our atoms were before us,
i wonder if they danced.

the poet's cake

i'm twenty-two and seeing myself to bed.
adult me decided that four pillows was the perfect amount,
though studies show it's a habit of loneliness.

i notice birthday paragraphs turned into just happy birthdays and love
yous.
the video tape of my dad on my 4th birthday wearing a witch's hat and
playing peekaboo
turned into a simple smile.

i suppose you grow tired of it all.
buying cards that write poetry for you to compensate for lack of words
because someone means so much you can't write.

repetition doesn't strike me.
so when i see a string of words,
a sentence or so,
that seem minuscule but mean galaxies,
i am moved in the way that a sunset tide drifts.

it's funny.
with every year my age dresses up,
this year in such beautiful colours,
i seem to be fuller and fuller on words.

i'm twenty-two and stuffed with poetry.
all i know is i'll keep growing older
but i'll forever be hungry
for the words i'll never be gifted.

april showers

denim sky
slips into something more comfortable;
night on the cusp of adorning day.

follow me through rain,
dipping toes into pools of prolongation,
stepping gently as you carry
buckets of overflowing tenderness.

wait with a mouthful of devotion
tucked between tongue and teeth;
may they soon spill through your gaze
into the palms of my hands and
into my lap.

let your fingers ache
like those of a pianist
figuring out his favourite chords
for the first time.
let them guide you to
honey buttercream skin,
embroidered with beauty spots
and all the saccharine places
only the sun has ever tasted.

my lover,
hold me remorselessly,
our heartbeats a medley melting entirely.

i'd like to get to know all of you
all at once.

stargaze

backs to middle country road, chasing dreams

as if we only had one night to make it.
winter wind a breathing teacher
reminding us we'll be okay, to never quit.
like mains in a coming-of-age feature.

endless fields of lush green. the ones laying
next to me and my friend stargazing.

it's too late to go home now we're not the same.
sometimes when i see the north star i feel sixteen again.
i still hold a picture too delicately agonising to frame.
when i put my phone in my jeans i want to feel the world
in the way i did back then.

perhaps i won't feel alignment like the sky.
perhaps i will find comfort in knowing even then
when it felt like we had nothing,
we found beauty up in everything to simply get by.

always at fifty-two

by the time you walk me home,
the countertops are drenched in laughter
from a ping-pong match of inside jokes.
it is soaked in secrets we spilled
beside salt and pepper shakers
and water rings under empty glasses.

it was 2am and i popped in
for a cheese sandwich. we
flooded the room
with weird songs and deep thoughts.
things we said through smiles
(like me simping over my mans)
decorated every inch of every wall
like paintings in an art gallery.

see, you may not know it but
because of you, i keep believing.
because of you, i feel alive
when before i was just dreaming.

when we went, you reminded me
not to forget my coat.
i think, *how have we known each other for just over a year*
but it feels like we always have?

you don't realise the light you emit,
how it spreads like a tide stretching onto sand.
it's inevitable that stars
are destined to find each other
in nights we are made to do more than survive,
in nights we were made to **live**.

itch i can't scratch

strangers look at me
as if i were an indecision
in broad daylight.

two-tone jeans
but they only asked for
one
crying, "I just wanted BLUE jeans."

strangers look at me
picking out parts of my DNA
like they're hunting for treasure among
dirt
too bad all that gold
never seems to amount to
enough

everyone looks at me
but they don't see
that after a lifetime of itching skin
i've grown too tired now
to scatch it all off
so i think i'll just sleep in it.

forsaken

constellations
kiss all the spaces
on my skin,

yet they splatter me
too far from
conspicuous.

how can i endear
all of my pieces;
even the jagged
and some kind of speculated?

one push
shatters the whole puzzle.
i am bereft,
left with fragments of who
i think or thought i am or was,
collapsing like imbalanced books in a school hallway.

arms flail for help as per.
my feet strangers to gravity,
a force only familiar with clarity.

galaxies breathe
behind my eyelids,
refused of past or value
too many times
too
intimidatingly vast.

notice
i wear shades of blue
to keep cool,
to blend in,
to feel as innate as water.

keeping my head
just above the surface
to whisper-
shh.

ripples won't resonate
but will create
unjustified noise.

all i can do is
at least try to breathe.
you'd think by now
i'd have got the hang of it.

stars aren't strangers

not once did i wish to be a comet
emitting a fluorescent dalliance.
though they are magnets to the eye,
they are not made for anyone.

not once did i wish for nocturnal novas
to drown in the floods of a brazen lamp
and become a bulb suffocated in darkness,
dimming over time.

yes, i have wished for freedom,
but i wish to fly and not to float.
perhaps all it takes is time
for the stars to strap to my shoulders.

not once did i wish to be discovered
fleeting in the lens of a telescopic eye.
so it seems they have heard my final wish;
not to be made for anyone but
made to be part of
someone's sky.

midnight hour

learn to let loose
and forget your shoes
at midnight.
leave them by the window ledge,
climb on the roof
and breathe the air
as if drawing oxygen for the first time.
air thick with drowsy dreams
and words that wouldn't feel right
to say any other time.

you're not going to be twenty again
in two weeks.
the years will pass us by
and moments will fleet and fly
and we'll have everything
except the memories we
didn't make time for.

so learn to let loose
and forget your shoes
at midnight.

there'll always be another pair,
and if not,
you better use your feet while you can.

so this is twenty-one

eventually i'll regret turning to rust too soon.
no, i'm not shiny and new:
this road is still something i'm getting used to.

you've got things to do.
i've got dreams to catch
and a blissful agony awaiting if they ever collapse.
i've got friends, we find stability
in one another's company.
i've got people who will talk to the ceiling
with me until 11pm turns to quarter past three.
i've got people who are with me but their eyes constantly watch the door.
because the world is knocking,
but i have a craving to explore.

i'm finding these fleeting moments now have little to give
so tell me; how can i write when i don't have time to just live?

a first time for everything

goosebumps like soldiers on skin,
an alliance of only wool and cotton layers
to sense.

i feel the poetry no longer simmering but
rotting somewhere inside of me.
somewhere biology cannot place a name.

winter's sharp exhale seems to invite its way into
every gap in my clothes,
and i think that maybe soon,
i will wither like a snowflake
that was made to melt.

i think that maybe soon,
i will realise that just because snowflakes
fall
they aren't always going to stick.

all i can notice
is that in the next beat of my heart,
half the strings of a harp
snapped
and died with dissonance.

midnight

midnights, camera, action

midnight.
being top secret
is sexy at first.
woman.
homewrecker-
without stepping foot in.

it is not my job to handle a man,
or handle a home without his helping hand.
it is not my job to sacrifice
the lights that illuminate within me.
it is not my fault
they dress me up to be the girl i'd dreamed.

every beam from my ambient room
tastes like gold laced peaches.
and better yet, taste like sticky sweet freedom,
sitting lightweight on the tip of my tongue
ready to melt.
no longer do i bathe in your shadow,
for i have outrun it.

how i write my story
is something a camera cannot capture.
poetry does not present a perfect angle
or a visually beautiful shot.
you yelled, cut.
decapitated my raw heart between clapperboard,
left your hands drenched red,
and our memories faded from sky blue to black.

midnight.
woman.
set-wrecker.
built it up for a year.
and it's not as if you left a trace of me
in the real world.
it's not as if i stepped foot in.

between me and you

if every sun spot was a kiss from you in the past life,
you would've loved me endlessly.
lips upon skin, gently in the hundreds,
because you couldn't just stop at three.

there, in the sunflower field
you used to meet me in your dreams,
we would've done it right.
there would be no distance or
late night fights-
maybe in that life
i wouldn't have countless pieces of change
hiding in my pockets.
maybe i wouldn't have to buy myself a locket
you would've lent me your coat, you would've
bought me flowers,
instead of discussing oscar winners and cinematics for hours
with everyone but me.

my love was too early for you then
and too late for you now.
after all, you'd be oblivious if you lost me in a crowd.

each time i reached out my hand,
i didn't know what i'd get,
and that final version of you was one i'd never met.
every interaction like a bag of pick and mix;
i fell hard for your treats
and even harder for your tricks.

now, my name isn't bob.
i'm not a builder,
and you aren't something i can fix.
but making you smile was a gift
i really,
really miss.

that being said, i know all of my friends will
hate me if i admit
that i really really wish
i didn't say goodbye.

if every sun spot was a kiss from you in the past life,
then my skin holds endless traces of you and i.
i guess it could've been us in this one
if you actually bothered to try.

late

why do people rush when they're late
but slow down when they're *too late?*

it is only too late if i run
and meet the finish line.

it is only too late if i become
so blissfully unaware
of a life spent competing against the arms of a clock.

last night all i knew was that i am yours and you are mine.

if you let go of my hand,

if you
            stopped,

if you   sprinted
   ,

i couldn't bear this road without you.

the sensitive one

two logs burning.
call it a kindle,
call it a camp,
call it an emergency;
either way there's a fire.

things that spread like orange-lit leaves in my heart
look like candlelight to many and a few.
when i pour my guts out,
i forget i'll never be able to scoop
all of it back up again and cram it down my throat whole.
instead, i swallow the air of a winter's day
and tell myself i'm full off an empty bowl.

i watch the wreckage it creates
when i give a lot of love,
yet feel i have little to take.

a match lit.
call it a spark,
call it a flame,
call a brigade;
either way, there's a fire.

immortalised

another year wasted
on someone's son.
another year blinded
by someone who i thought was the one.

he had his priorities-
friends and food and a big screen
way above my company;
evidently my love wasn't good enough
for the likes of a hollywood scene.

if his selfish messes and destruction
cause him any heartache at all,
maybe his views on women will sway
but i'll know forever that he disrespected
the one who was hardest to fall.

he might hate this book.
he might hate me.
but this is my time now
to show him what happens when i break free.
once i choose myself instead of staying
i will show him exactly what happens
when i leave.

we can't go to the beach, for there's a storm

you like beautiful, beautiful, beautiful sunbeams.
you like the ocean.
the way waves rush to your feet,
the way salt air replenishes your lungs.
the way footpath and water never meet.

you love the solid support of sand.
dainty shells, smooth to touch.
silk skinned pebbles to skim over and over,
monotony never getting too much.

over, and over, and over,
hour after hour, your mind watches
and sometimes swims.
but too far and surroundings turn to splotches,
so every time, you desperately cling
to the closest thing beneath your feet.
never going too far,
caution over freedom, can't handle being behind
the wheel of a car.
but let me tell you;

staying close to safety
is staying miles away from your furthest dreams.
staying close to safety
turns on warning lights in place of your screams.
staying close to safety
is losing everything you take for granted,
like beautiful, beautiful, beautiful sunbeams.

Beneath the Blue

Written by Karishma Natu
-
Illustrated by Victoria Grant

"This book is a movie, bro."
-Ben Whittall

About Karishma Natu

Karishma Natu is a twenty-two year old poet, born and raised in Devon, UK. During her time at Arts University Bournemouth, she hand-crafted two poetry chapbooks, which were shared with friends, family, and her community. Since graduating and getting her bachelor's degree in Creative Writing, she has created a growing space for her words on TikTok and brought this book to life. Karishma spends her time out in nature, baking cookies, and singing like a walking jukebox. Oh, and of course, she is never without a pen.

ISBN: 978-1-3999-7105-8

Socials:

Instagram– @karishmapoetry
Tiktok– @karidaydreams

Acknowledgments

A huge thank you to:

- My family, for putting up with me and letting me follow the path to my dreams.

-My illustrator and amazing friend, Victoria, for making this dream come true. INFJ's for the win.

-My dear beautiful friends. You know who you are. I'm so grateful to have you in my life.

-The boy that last broke my heart. You taught me that a cup of tea can mend most things. You inspired me to continue to grow as a better lover, and a better writer.

-James (my uni course leader) for teaching me, creating the course that changed my life for the better, and being a huge part of my journey as a poet.

-Charlie and Malcolm for hosting my book launch, employing me, and above all, believing in me.

-Reader, for buying this book! Your support means tremendous amounts to me. I hope you found warmth and safety in my words. Keep going, keep going, keep going.

9 781399 971058